# CHAPTER 1

# WHY ARE WE LOST IN TRANSMISSION?

*In business, communication is everything.*

—ROBERT KENT,
*the former dean of the Harvard Business School*

It seems so easy. In order to sell a product or a service, we need to communicate. Or, to put it more scientifically, a sender and receiver must share an idea using one of many communication channels.

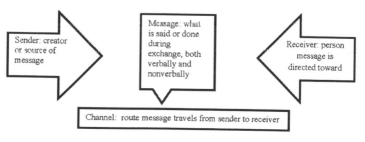

Adapted from *Basic Elements and Tips to Build Effective Workplace Communication* by Amanda-Makenzi Braedyn Svecz.

With only four components, the process of communication would be simple and straightforward. But ask any manager, executive, business owner, or employee what the greatest hurdle is to making a living, and the answer you'll get, hands down, is "communication."

The problem is not communication in and of itself, but communicating consistently, efficiently, and effectively across channels. While that's always been something we could improve, in the last decade the challenge has become much more demanding.

I've noticed it almost daily in my work as a professional development consultant. In fact, in the last several years, *every* company I've worked with—every single one—has asked for coaching and training programs to help them communicate more effectively. These are some of the questions I hear constantly:

- "What's the most streamlined way to share information internally?"

- "How can we make sure our managers are delegating work in a way their employees understand?"

- "What's the best way to communicate with our clients?"

- "What can we do to ensure everyone in the organization is on the same page in terms of mission?"

- "How do I manage the high volume of information I get each day?"

- Or simply "How can we communicate better?"

So, although it seems like such an easy thing to do — express an idea and have your recipient get the message — in truth, it's pretty complex.

## THE COMPLEXITIES OF COMMUNICATION

The problem, as you may have guessed, is the *way* we communicate, especially in recent years. It's not that the components of communication have changed — it's that each one has become more complex. Let's take a look:

- **Sender/Receiver:** Today, unlike any other time in history, people from widely diverse backgrounds, generations, and cultures are interacting through business. Because cultures and age groups communicate differently — whether that means the language they use or their style, tone, body language, or perspective — human differences can cause misunderstanding.

- **Message:** Content can be as varied in personality as the people delivering it. How do you present yourself? Will you be formal or informal, detailed or brief, use lots of industry jargon or speak plainly? Even the font and punctuation you choose can make a difference in how your message is received. With every message sent, communicators need to examine the circumstances and consider their choices carefully.

- **Channel:** Gone are the days when you either picked up the phone or left delivery to the postal service. Technology has changed all that. Now there's e-mail, texting, video conferencing, social networks, Websites, and a host of other options. This is perhaps the most challenging of all the aspects of modern communication: we have *so* many choices — and they're changing every day. It can be hard to keep up — and even harder to adapt.

## And the Sheer Quantity

But it's not just the complexity of people, messages, and channels that's increasing. Though I probably don't need to tell you, it's the volume.

Information overload is one of the biggest issues I've observed, both for the people and companies I work with and in the literature I read. Technology has made it incredibly easy to find and share information with e-mails, attachments, links, embedded photos, video, and so on. Matrixed work environments, where employees work on multiple projects for multiple bosses (all of which result in associated meetings), add to the mix. Managing the deluge of information is where I find people need the most help.

The volume of information can become over-whelming — no matter what kind of business you're in - and may weigh down even the strongest of employees. I work with all different types of com-panies — digital space, entertainment, health care, retail, and manufacturing — and through those experiences I've seen some common challenges and common themes, whether there are twenty thousand employees in the organization or two hundred.

Take, for example, a gentleman I work with as an executive coach. He is the CEO of a company with about 130 employees in five locations, so he has a lot to juggle. As you might expect, his e-mail volume is pretty high — somewhere between 250 and 300 e-mails a day. Each one of them needs his attention, whether that means reading an attached report, or making a decision on data that's been sent to him, or just understanding something for future reference. But the volume can understand-ably be overwhelming — to the point that he has trouble knowing where to even start. In fact, when he is finally able to sit down at the end of the day and attack the e-mails he hasn't yet responded to, there are days when he'd just like to throw up his hands and declare bankruptcy on his inbox. But of course, he can't. And tomorrow there'll be another three hundred waiting for him. And so on. And so on.

Together we've worked on finding ways to prioritize what ends up in his inbox and manage whether or not he receives that information in the first place. Using examples found in chapters 2 and 3 of this book, I've helped him devise a system to keep from feeling so overwhelmed — and from just hitting Delete All.

## Don't Get Lost in Transmission

Helping my clients avoid becoming lost in transmission is what led me to write this book.

Though it may not always seem that way, ongoing changes to the way we communicate were meant to be constructive and not destructive; to contribute to our success in business, not complicate it.

In my many years coaching individuals and organizations on ways to improve their productivity — especially the last ten — I've watched communication become a major roadblock. This book was created to offer practical advice on how to navigate through the profusion of channels, messages, and communicators you encounter daily, and find a system to help you achieve success — and still get some occasional sleep.

THIS BOOK WAS CREATED TO OFFER PRACTICAL ADVICE ON HOW TO NAVIGATE THROUGH THE PROFUSION OF CHANNELS, MESSAGES, AND COMMUNICATORS YOU ENCOUNTER DAILY, AND FIND A SYSTEM TO HELP YOU ACHIEVE SUCCESS— AND STILL GET SOME OCCASIONAL SLEEP.

## THE FIVE RECENT CHANGES

There are five recent changes that have greatly impacted workplace communication and which will be the focus of this book:

1. Information overload
2. E-mail as the most used and abused form of business communication
3. A workforce that includes four generations
4. Virtual work environments
5. Globalization

## INFORMATION OVERLOAD

Information overload, as I've already touched on, is a major contributor to communication problems. The ease with which individuals and organizations can share information—from vital reports to blind sales pitches to online coupons and social media posts—means that a constant river of information, including prize-winning catches flows your way. Added to that is 24/7 access, thanks to smart phones, PDAs, tablets, and laptops. The expectations that come from this situation—between manager and subordinate, client and account rep—can cause major challenges. In chapter 2, I'll highlight the demands brought on by information overload and provide some practical advice for how to address them.

## E-MAIL USE AND ABUSE

E-mail is probably the largest adjustment any company has had to make in terms of how its employees communicate, simply because everyone is using it. The challenges of e-mail range from appropriately targeting your audience and staying consistent with your company's culture to maintaining client confidentiality and avoiding "CYA (cover your ass) syndrome." In this chapter, I'll offer practical tips for how to put a stop to e-mail excesses as well as how to write the most effective e-mail to ensure, as much as you can, that it will be read.

## MULTIGENERATIONAL WORKFORCE

For the first time in history, four generations are sharing office buildings and factory floors across the country. Each group has its own style of interaction, and they don't always jibe with one another. In chapter 4, I'll delve into the difference in communication styles among veterans, baby boomers, generation Xers, and millennials and discuss ways to bring these various age groups together successfully despite their varying modes of interaction. (Of all the seminars I give, this was my most requested last year).

## VIRTUAL WORK ENVIRONMENT

The virtual work environment has exploded in the last five years, whether that means people working from home, in a satellite office, or from their hotel room or a coffee shop. In some cases, workers are expected to maintain a completely virtual office and don't even have an assigned space within their company's office building — in other words, pick a cube, any cube. Though unassigned offices are not the norm, virtual work is, and it offers many advantages. The downside can be how to develop a team philosophy when team members don't inhabit the same physical space, and how to ensure accountability without the expectation of 24/7 work. In chapter 5, I'll discuss how to overcome the challenges of working with people across town or even across the globe, how to balance work and home life when your office door is just down the hall, and some of the technical and virtual etiquette challenges that arise for virtual workers.

## GLOBALIZATION

Technology has allowed companies in every industry to increasingly extend their reach outside the United States, opening satellite offices, outsourcing departments, and providing products and services to clients in new parts of the world. Learning another country's language is just the first step in communicating well with your foreign counterparts and customers. Cultural differences vary widely across the globe, and in order to succeed in an international marketplace, it's imperative that you do your homework. In chapter 6, I'll provide examples of what you should be mindful of, offer tips for best practices, and give you tools for further research.

* * *

With twenty-first century technological advances, the resulting communication and work options available to us, and an ever-expanding workforce and customer base, it can be hard to avoid getting lost in a sea of channels, messages, senders, and receivers. Gone are the days when new tools came our way slowly and surely, giving us plenty of time to adapt. But we can't forget that this brave new world of communication options offers us huge advantages to past work styles, from faster project development and broader audiences to more diverse, creative workforces. To use modern communication to its best advantage, we need to examine the changes that have taken place, look at the challenges that have resulted from those changes, and find solutions to the issues.

Let's get started.

# Chapter 2

# Information Overload

*There comes a point where you have to decide
which information to look at and which
information to overlook.*

—Psychologist Robert Butterworth

It's a normal day at the office.

You sit down at your desk to see what the day
has in store. Outlook opens to reveal seventy-five
new e-mails. You start to scan, noticing twenty-two
of them are marked urgent, fourteen belong in the
CYA category, six appear to be newsletters, and
many are embedded with links or include attachments. Your IM window pops up—it's account-
ing, with a question about the quarterly report
you prepared. You click open Excel and the company database to reconcile figures, and begin to
type responses when your phone rings. It's your

colleague two cubicles down. Letting that go to voice mail, you finish the IM, and then open up your meeting calendar to check the day's schedule. Blocked solid from eight to four. Those e-mails will have to wait. Checking *Project,* you see you have three deadlines, one for each of your managers, all due on Wednesday. You stop for a moment, stare at the screen with all its open applications, and accept that it's going to be another long week. Picking up your BlackBerry with plans to tackle a few e-mails during your first morning meeting, you head down the hallway to the conference room.

\* \* \*

Sound familiar? In the last ten years, over-scheduling has become the regular routine of millions of people — sorting through a continuous stream of information from multiple channels, balancing a schedule filled with meetings from a variety of departments, constant interruptions and detours as new requests suddenly appear, and multitasking as a way of life.

For many, the flow of information has reached a tipping point.

## An Interesting Dilemma

Our love of technology and desire for information have presented us with an interesting dilemma.

Everyone is excited about the sleek toys, the incredible connection speed, and the great software and apps. There's always something new to covet and buy. And the need to be reachable fed by feeling valued and needed has its addictive quality too — it gives you a sense of importance, competence, even exhilaration. It's hard to control the technology and not let the technology control you. Data have shown that information workers check their e-mail an average of fifty times a day, usually within six seconds of a message's arrival. Psychologically, there's a feeling that you are making progress every time you hear that inbox chime.

> *Information workers check their e-mail on average fifty times per day, usually within six seconds of a message's arrival.*

But as we all know, there's another side to the story. E-mail, along with the many other ways we accumulate and share information digitally, is growing at an exponential pace. Between 2005 and 2010 alone, the amount of information created, captured, and replicated worldwide grew tenfold. The information can take the form of written content, images, video, and audio — all, of course, transmittable in an instant to your handheld device.

Because it's so easy to access, send, and deliver, information has taken on a life of its own. And though we may savor being ultraconnected, the nonstop flow of data can also make us stressed, unfocused, and even sick.

## THE CHALLENGE OF CONTINUOUS INTERRUPTION

There's a good reason we feel overloaded by information. Information delivery is actually moving at a pace that exceeds our physical ability to adequately absorb it. The constant onslaught of e-mail and other forms of real-time communication delivery are challenging for the human brain because the brain does not work well with constant interruptions. Consider that corporate employees received between fifty and two hundred e-mails a day in 2009 and that didn't even include texts, phone and cellular calls, IMs, or video conferencing.

To properly engage, we actually require significantly more processing time than is allowed by our new technologies. For example, studies have shown that it takes eight uninterrupted minutes to get into a creative state—and the typical office worker is interrupted every three.

> *It takes eight uninterrupted minutes to get into a creative state—and the typical office worker is interrupted every three.*

It also takes longer to get back on track once you've been pulled away to read a text, follow a link, or scroll through messages. Gloria Mark, a professor from the University of California-Irvine whose research examines how high-tech devices affect human behavior, has measured how long it takes for an interrupted office worker to return to his or her original task—a surprising twenty-five minutes. This start-and-stop work approach makes us inefficient—even though it might feel like we're getting a lot done when we multitask. On top of that, constant interruption adds to the fact that most of us are notoriously unrealistic at setting realistic time frames for completing tasks.

## A Matrix Environment

The matrix environment a lot of companies work within adds another wrinkle to how people interact with information.

One of the clients I work with that uses the matrix structure is an online company that's tripled in size in the last four years. Instead of having a vertical chain of command, employees work for multiple managers on multiple projects. It's a pretty common structure for project-heavy industries like tech companies.

The challenge comes from the amount of communication required for each project, the need for the team to focus on the big picture as well as the details, and shifting priorities from management. If the managers overseeing the same talent pool don't communicate well with one another, political dams can form. A lot of the companies working in a matrix environment are growing quickly, too, just like the organization I mentioned. That means staffing might not be keeping up with workload, with its deeper layers of information to sort through and manage. I've heard often from the employees at this particular company that the expectations for the people doing the work can be unrealistic.

The time required for meetings can also quickly get out of hand. One client I coach literally has her Outlook calendar booked from 9:00 a.m. until 7:00 p.m. with in-person meetings, conference calls, and planning sessions. To get any of her work done, she ends up staying at the office as late as 10:00 p.m. every night. Together, we're working on a way to manage her day so that she has blocks of quiet time between nine and five to tackle her objectives and allow her some work–life balance.

## THE MODERN DESKTOP DILEMMA

I consult for one prestigious digital media client that has a reputation for producing effectivesoftware.Unfortunately, it is actually plagued by internal communication issues and at times fall victim to the very

*Software applications were actually designed to compete for our attention.*

products that made them a success. Paradoxically, the very virtual desktops and multiple applications running simultaneously that are designed to improve efficiency can ultimately interfere with organizational efficiency.

Software applications were actually designed to compete for our attention. At any given time, the average person has multiple applications open simultaneously — Outlook, Google, a Word doc, the office database — layered with popup reminders for meetings, IMs, inbox status messages, and so on. The overwhelming amount of information can lead to what psychologist Edward Hallowell calls "attention deficit trait" — skimming along the surface of many different pools of information without fully immersing yourself in any one.

Martin Mann is a time management expert whose website http://www.43folders.com offers great articles and tips for managing your inbox and cutting out unnecessary information. He suggests that workers should "accept that your workload exceeds your resources — that you are the first and last filter for what deserves your time — and (by filtering out what comes across your desktop) ... you'll already be better off than you were even two minutes ago." Not all messages carry the same amount of importance, and some are "like a Christmas present that must be savored," Mann writes. You need to become ruthless in what you are able to look at, and when you are able to spend time with it.

## COMPANY AND INDIVIDUAL HEALTH

When we learn to manage information overload, we become more agile, responsive, and efficient workers, and contribute more significantly to our company's bottom lines. We also become more physically and mentally healthy — and that's nothing to sneeze at. Before turning to practical techniques for mitigating information overload, let's look briefly to how it impacts organization's and individual's health.

## ORGANIZATIONAL EFFECTS

Productivity has started to waver because of information overload, and companies are paying the price. According to the LexisNexis 2010 International Workplace Survey, eight in ten professionals admit to deleting or discarding work information without fully reading and processing the material.

The data reveal that workers

- aren't reading crucial reports
- are delivering incomplete documents due to lack of readily accessible information
- miss appointments and meetings because of scheduling miscommunication
- experience trouble re-creating how time was spent for billing purposes

Staffing reductions in a tight economy are another part of the picture. More work and more stress have been added to each position, and there's a hesitation to approach the boss and look for solutions when your job could be on the line.

## PHYSICAL AND MENTAL TOLLS

David Shenk, a well-known expert on information overload, pinpoints some of the symptoms brought on by information overload, cited from various psychological studies spanning thirty years:

- Increased cardiovascular stress, due to a rise in blood pressure

- Weakened vision

- Impaired judgment based on overconfidence

- Decreased benevolence to others due to an "environmental input glut"

Researchers are also investigating the connection between the electromagnetic radiation emitted by cell phones and such diseases as cancer, Alzheimer's disease, and Parkinson's, though it's still too early to tell if there's a link.

## THE COSTS TO RELATIONSHIPS

Our relationships and social lives are also taking a hit, not only because we're so often distracted by technology when we're with family and friends — an iPhone on the table beside us at dinner, a laptop open on our blanket at the beach — but also because of the difficulty in conveying tone and emotion when we're dashing off e-mails and texts left and right.

Dr. Alex Lickerman writes about the effects of technology and relationships, and his assessment gets right to the heart of the matter: "We may feel we're connecting effectively with others via the Internet, but too much electronic-relating paradoxically engenders a sense of social isolation."

Dr. Lickerman points out the difficulties of conveying joy and human connection when messaging, and the ease with which confrontation is expressed under the neutral guise of a blog post or text.

> "We may feel we're connecting effectively with others via the Internet, but too much electronic-relating paradoxically engenders a sense of social isolation."
> — Alex Lickerman, MD

Even compliments can be misconstrued. One of my clients is a strong leader with a sarcastic sense of humor that doesn't always translate well on-screen. She recently sent a text to one of her employees complimenting him on a project he'd just finished. She closed it with "You're such a slacker!" — clearly a wisecrack in her mind, but he had no idea how to read the comment. After some uncomfortable moments they sorted it out, and she felt bad about the confusion. This innocent remark goes to show how easily meaning can be lost in transmission.

Silence can also be a dangerous thing. You send an e-mail, do not receive a timely response, and you start to wonder: "Did they get it?" "Are they ignoring me?" "Is this some sort of power play?" Or "Are they just overwhelmed, like me?"

## TOOLS AND TECHNIQUES TO ADDRESS INFORMATION OVERLOAD

So now let's get down to brass tacks: how to deal with information overload and prevent it from degrading the quality of your work or taking over every waking moment of your life.

There are three main categories for managing information: behavior modification, company-enforced boundaries, and technology. Depending on your industry, your organizational culture, and your individual work style and personality, some of these tips and techniques will work for you; others may not. You may find you are already using some of these techniques but want to reexamine and tweak them—or take a whole new approach. Give yourself time to see if various methods work well for you and are sustainable. Consistency is key.

## BEHAVIOR MODIFICATION

It can be hard to pull yourself out of a well-worn routine, but just as behavior modification can help someone quite smoking or improve eating habits, it can help liberate someone who is a slave to his or her BlackBerry.

## SCHEDULE, SCHEDULE, SCHEDULE

➢ Though it may seem almost too obvious to mention, having **a consistent schedule for work** is one of the best ways you can take control of your time and refuse to let interruptions drive what you do. Set aside specific break and lunch times, and leave your desk when the clock strikes. Make a point to turn off or leave behind your PDA or smart phone. Arrive and leave at the same hours each day, as much as that's possible. This schedule will group your day into measurable time frames that will help you control how work is managed and completed.

➢ **Make a to-do list every day** if you aren't doing so already. Be realistic about the time it takes to complete tasks, knowing that some interruptions are inevitable, and work at blocking out dedicated chunks of time for deep thinking. This can be done electronically, by using a daily planner, or even in a notebook. The important point is that you have a to-do list and you use it. Many people find this process of making this list helpful because it can transform a seemingly unclimbable mountain of work into a series of doable tasks.

➢ **Do your most important tasks first**, when your mind is at its best. This will give you a feeling of accomplishment daily, which will energize you for the rest of your to-do list. A University of London study for Hewlett-Packard determined that your brain's highest capacity is in the early morning, before levels of noradrenaline and dopamine have increased in response to the introduction of new stimuli. When those neurotransmitter levels become too high, "complex thinking becomes more difficult, making it harder to make decisions and solve problems." Therefore, your early morning hours are much better spent on complex activities.

> **Reset your e-mail settings so** only your work related e-mails come through: if you are able to create a filter so that your friends and family e-mails only come through mid-morning, midafternoon, and at the end of the day, that may help you reduce distractions. This is a hard one, but very effective if you have the willpower and your work flow allows it. As much as it may tempt you to hit Send/Receive throughout the day, learn to avoid that urge.

> **Make coworkers aware of your new approach to e-mail,** and ask them to respect it. They will need to be reminded, but after a while will change their expectations from immediate responsiveness to a more manageable schedule.

## MODE OF COMMUNICATION

➤ **Choose one way you will receive the bulk of your information**, and stick to it. E-mail is the easiest to manage and the easiest for others to use as a single way to communicate with you. Let your network know what you are doing, and avoid the siren's call of other communication modes. Obviously there will be times you have to respond to phone calls and texts, for example, but do your best to have a centralized means of communicating with others and a set time for doing it.

➤ **Consider having a separate computer monitor dedicated to e-mail.** If you dedicate one monitor to work and the other to e-mail, you can much more easily compartmentalize work and communication tasks. Keeping the e-mail computer out of your line of vision will also help you ignore it when you are performing creative work.

➤ **Calibrate the settings on your PDA to help you manage e-mail.** Some people prefer to have e-mails they delete on their BlackBerry remain on their PC, where they can attack them later. Some like them deleted from both simultaneously. It's up to your comfort level and work style. I find that I use my BlackBerry to quickly scan e-mails to gauge their level of importance, and then use my desktop to respond to the more in-depth messages when I get back to the office. To me, it can be challenging to elegantly compose and format a long and detailed e-mail with thumbs on a tiny keyboard.

## FILTERS

> **Start prioritizing your e-mails with filters.** Create holding folders for all the second- (or third- or fourth-) tier e-mail you receive that you don't need to look at immediately but that you also don't want to junk. This would include trade newsletters, LinkedIn requests, press releases, etc. Flag those senders so their messages drop into those folders, then set aside afternoon time two or three times a week to go through that information.

> **Limit the number of news sites, trade publications, and blogs you subscribe to/look at each day.** Ask yourself what value you are getting from each, and then be ruthless in cutting out those that don't contribute to your job directly. Schedule when you read the ones that float to the top of the list, as you would any other category of information. Reprioritize as you become aware of new sites, and try to replace rather than add to the collection of information sources you view.

➢ **Filter the people you communicate with.** We all have colleagues and friends who send us jokes, videos, or unnecessary information, or who copy us on practically every e-mail they send. Ask them to stop, repeatedly if necessary. And monitor yourself so you aren't doing the same to others.

➢ **Filter your archives.** It's tempting to save every piece of information you get, but much of it we never read again. Each time you receive an e-mail, ask yourself if you can get the information from another source, if it is a priority, or if it's associated with a deadline. If not, delete it. You'll be surprised how much you can filter.

## TIME OUT

➢ In addition to allotting yourself spans of uninterrupted time, **consider using a separate physical space to do essential work.** Conference rooms, unused offices, or company libraries are all options. If the space is reserved by schedule, all the better. Putting your name down for a set period of time will help you focus on a single task. Then leave behind your devices and turn off Outlook on your laptop while you're there. You can leave an automated "I'm unavailable" message for incoming e-mails so colleagues and clients don't think you're ignoring them.

> **If working with a team, try to unplug together.** There's nothing more distracting or impolite than people answering phone calls and e-mail on their BlackBerries during a meeting or when teamwork is required. You can ask that people leave their devices at their desks or on a table near the door to encourage focused time together. When teaching a seminar I establish this expectation up front, letting participants know I will allow them BlackBerry/bio breaks every hour. Unless they work for the medical industry, where receiving an e-mail really *could* mean the difference between life and death, we all agree that most of us can unplug for twenty or thirty minutes to focus on a meeting.

> **Communicate in person.** It seems crazy to e-mail the coworker in the cubicle next to yours, but it happens all the time. Face-to-face conversations can be much more effective, and will clear out your inbox that much more. Schedule them as you would e-mail time, so you take care of them all at once, whenever possible.

## COMPANY-ENFORCED BOUNDARIES

Businesses, concerned about the toll information overload has on their employees as well as their bottom lines, are starting to put practices into place to help quell the tide. Some ideas that might work for your company include:

> **Create companywide guidelines on e-mail use.** Drafting company guidelines to prevent e-mail abuse is a fairly simple thing to do. Bullet points could include keeping e-mails short and to the point, summarizing necessarily long e-mails in the first three lines of the document, and copying only the most essential people. And perhaps most importantly, always create a meaningful subject line. For detailed suggestions, see chapter 3. The key to guidelines succeeding is reinforcing them as practices start to inevitably slip.

> **E-mail-free times.** A major software company's marketing department put this idea to work one day a week—Fridays—with great success. The department's executive VP suggested the move in response to receiving a daily inundation of four hundred e-mails per employee, many from staff members. It isn't a wholesale ban—employees still respond to customers and staff from other departments that day—but for internal e-mails, department members are encouraged to find another way to communicate. The move has reduced e-mails by half on Fridays, and has had a carryover effect of decreasing the number of messages popping into employee's inboxes the rest of the week, too.

➢ **Set aside quiet times for employees.** Just as individuals can schedule themselves for unplugged time alone or with workgroups, companies can encourage focused work periods by institutionalizing this process.

➢ **Before applying a new technology, figure out how the technology can best be incorporated into the workplace.** It's easy to jump on the bandwagon every time a new technology appears, adding one more layer to the information employees must manage each day. If management considers how the technology will be integrated before IT loads it onto employee desktops or installs an app onto PDA's, there is a much greater likelihood of successful implementation.

➢ **Manage how information is distributed.** Most companies have central storage options for information, so that shared content would be effectively organized and maintained. Unfortunately, many employees circumvent the central storage solution and instead, create information redundancies by storing the same information on their local drives. To better manage the distribution process, company IT departments can institute training for all new and existing employees on shared information locations and insist that they be used. Establishing a company Shared Drive or using third party applications such as Microsoft's SharePoint can improve collaboration by allowing multiple users to access, view, and edit files while limiting the number of document versions.

## SPEAK UP WHEN THE DELUGE GETS OUT OF HAND

> Employees need to **communicate with managers** when the number of e-mails and meetings get out of hand and getting down to work becomes unachievable. This is especially true in matrix environments. Be sure to go to your boss(es) with solutions rather than just to complain. Perhaps you can ask that they triage the level of detail you receive on each project or suggest that project managers coordinate and prioritize deadlines more often, communicating decisions clearly to staff. If you don't have effective project management software in place, taking the time to establish an effective platform can be very helpful. Hiring and training a person dedicated to maintaining schedules and filtering communication might also be a solution.

## TECHNOLOGY

Technology commonly solves its own problems with more technology, and the same is true for electronic communication. A number of software programs have come out in recent years to help deal with the influx in our inboxes. Because this is an ever-changing arena, I have described generally some of the tools currently available so you can research options further.

> **E-mail management software that assign "postage" to e-mails**. This new concept in software could be useful in breaking employees of their bad habit of sending too many e-mails. Depending on the number of recipients, the length of the e-mail, its urgency, and other parameters, postage is assigned to the e-mail and is "paid for" out of a user's virtual postage account. The more detailed the message, the higher the rate, leading senders to think more carefully before they press Send.

> **Filtering software**. These programs check to see who the sender is and calculate his or her importance in relation to your past e-mail activity with this person or their place in the company hierarchy. It also analyzes how busy you are based on your computer activity. Urgent messages are delivered directly to your inbox; less-important messages are prioritized for later delivery.

> **Integration software.** This software supplies the user with contact information and communication history about the sender from a variety of sources — Facebook, LinkedIn, and

archived texts, e-mails, and calls. Senders are ranked according to importance based on this data.

> **Color-coded software.** In early studies of how information is most effectively presented to astronauts, researcher Mary Czerwinski discovered that visual graphics incorporating color most effectively clued recipients into the level of a message's importance to professionals in high-stress situations. (Text was easy to ignore because it blended in with all of the other directions astronauts were receiving onscreen.) This generation of software works with that idea in mind, sorting e-mails using color to indicate their importance and topic, and grouping associated tasks: meetings contacts, for example. At a glance, users can determine who is sending the e-mail, where it fits within their project assignments, and how urgent the need is to respond.

## Take Charge

We're all creatures of habit, and because we are now immersed in and surrounded by technology 24/7, we sometimes get the sense that we are controlled by the technology, rather than vice versa. Technology should be a tool, not a commanding force in our daily actions — as Pavlovian as it can make us act. Once you manage that tool, you can put it into its proper perspective as something that helps you instead of controls you. The big payoff is that downtime will once again become a part of life. You are in control of your use of electronics and preventing the overload, be the master and not the victim.

# CHAPTER 3

# E-MAIL: THE MOST USED AND ABUSED FORM OF COMMUNICATION

*89.1% of the 294 billion e-mails
sent in 2010 were SPAM*

- ROYAL PINGDOM

If there's one form of communication the majority of people use at work, no matter what their age or circumstances, it's e-mail. They may not text, IM, videoconference, or use a company intranet, but just about everyone sends and receives e-mail on a daily basis. That's why e-mail has become the major culprit in our information-overloaded era.

Though there may be days we wish our over-filled inboxes would just disappear, e-mail is here to stay. Even with the introduction of new ways to share information, e-mail holding steady as the channel of choice for information workers. The Radicati Group recently projected where e-mail is headed as other types of communication using a keyboard and an Internet connection gain more and more popularity—namely social networking and instant messaging. They discovered that e-mail is growing as steady a rate as social and IM, and may in fact be staying ahead of the pack. The chart below shows the number of e-mail users world-wide in billions, and projected trends into the second decade of the twenty-first century:

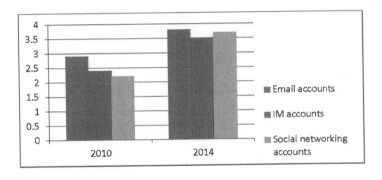

Data source: The Radicati Group, *E-Mail Statistics Report*, 2010.

## WHY IS E-MAIL SO POPULAR?

There are many good reasons. First and foremost, e-mail is a really effective way of communicating. Whether your message is big or small, electronic communication works great: You can use e-mail to dash off a short note or to send a highly complex multipage report with embedded images or even video. And electronic mail is very efficient. No matter how many people you need to include as recipients, sending your message is practically instantaneous. Unlike phone calls or meetings, e-mail also provides a written record that's easy to refer to later—which is one of its main advantages (and, if you're not careful, a major liability, as we've learned from a number of corporate leaders and politicians).

E-mail communication has many advantages, or it wouldn't maintain its standing as the favored communication channel. In a 2010 survey done for the Pew Internet and American Life Project, workers gave e-mail high ratings. Here are some of the reasons they gave, all of which fell above the forty-third percentile, many in the seventieth:

- E-mail is the most effective way to make **appointments** and get **last-minute details** out quickly.

- It keeps **large numbers** of widely dispersed employees **informed**.

- E-mail makes **reviewing and editing documents efficient**, bypassing cumbersome practices of faxing, copying, and mailing.

- It **improves teamwork** by enhancing information and work flow.

- E-mail makes people feel they know one another by **strengthening social ties**.

- It can be used to **flatten hierarchies** by allowing high-level managers to communicate with thousands of employees in the organization.

No wonder we find e-mail so useful.

## E-MAIL AND GLOBALIZATION

Another advantage of e-mail is that it makes the world smaller in our globalized workplace.

Any time, day or night, e-mail is always available to us when we need to communicate with overseas clients and customers. And even better, it's cheap — especially in comparison to the phone calls, snail mail, or overnight delivery methods we relied on in the past. Translation software can even break down language barriers — and is bringing cultures together like never before.

## THE CHALLENGE

So what are the downsides? I'm guessing you might have a few ideas.

Though survey results from the Pew Research Center project came back with positive reactions to e-mail topping the list, its disadvantages were also clear:

- E-mail is **too accessible to others**, putting it at a disadvantage for private interactions.

- The constant interruptions caused by e-mail are **a distraction from work.**

- Because of its volume, e-mail is a **source of stress.**

- **Tone** can be an issue on e-mail, causing **misunderstandings.**

- This silent form of communication **encourages gossip.**

On the whole, people took the bad with the good, as this chart showing overall attitudes toward e-mail reveals:

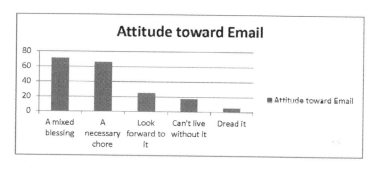

Data source: Pew Internet and American Life Project, 2010.

In my personal experience, the data do not lie. Clients name these same advantages and challenges in the professional e-mail courses I teach. They're looking for ways to optimize the best assets of e-mail while avoiding the worst.

## MAKE IT WORK

A key problem is the effectiveness of each individual e-mail you send.

In the companies I work with, which include very well-established organizations in traditional sectors such as banking and manufacturing and younger industries like new media, approaches to e-mail format vary widely. Company culture drives the formality or informality of e-mails. And that can greatly impact how well it works.

As a general rule, I've noticed that the traditional organizations tend to have more stringent expectations — they'd like their employees' e-mails to be very bottom-lined and targeted, with body copy supporting the subject line, in a letter or memo format. Companies newer to the scene lean toward a more informal style, with smaller amounts of information in each message, sometimes even incorporating text-message shorthand. Even when using shorthand, a good rule of thumb is to never leave a subject line empty, because it helps alert the reader to the message's content, importance, and makes it easier to search for in the future.

While it's important for companies to maintain a personality suited to their industry — I never recommend a boilerplate style for e-mail — shorter and more conversational is not always better. Good examples of when not to use an informal style are open-loop or blocking e-mails.

## OPEN LOOPS AND BLOCKING

An open loop occurs when a sender offers too many options in an e-mail, or asks too many questions, making it nearly impossible to resolve all the queries in one reply. For example:

To: Chelsea Johnson
From: David Newman
Subject: Questions
Hi Chelsea,
Let's get together to talk about the Halburn project this week. When would you like to meet? We could get together Monday, Wednesday, or Friday, unless you have a day that would work better? What time would be good for you? I was thinking we could either meet at our boardroom or grab a cup of coffee at Starbucks on 6$^{th}$ — or do you like the one on Glendale better?
Looking forward to hearing from you,
Dave
P.S. We should also make plans to go over the schedule for the Auburn project. Any ideas?

Dave has made it just about impossible for Chelsea to handle this e-mail in a single response. The two of them are in for multiple back-and-forths — just to set a date to meet. It's a classic case of the open loop.

Blocking is similarly inefficient and frustrating. I recently dealt with a situation similar to this:

To: Jane Smith
From: Kathy Sprager
Subject: Meeting to discuss new logo
Jane,
I'm available to discuss your new logo on Thursday at 11, 12, or 1. Do any of these times work for you?
Kathy

To: Kathy Sprager
From: Jane Smith
Subject: RE: Meeting to discuss new logo
No.

The reply would almost be funny, if it weren't so inefficient. These two spent several follow-up e-mails coming to a consensus on the date for this meeting. A few thoughtful minutes of time on the recipient's part, and a successful resolution could have been achieved within three e-mails.

## MUCH TOO MUCH

Poor planning when composing e-mail messages makes for a lot of wasted time and effort, and a lot more e-mails. And as we explored earlier, excessive volume and frequency are the main complaints people have with modern communication.

There is a threshold to what we can handle and still get our work done. Survey results from Harris Interactive put the breaking point at fifty e-mails per day.

To some of you, that may seem like a light load—many of my clients receive hundreds of e-mails a day. But responding to just fifty e-mails can take hours, depending the length and complexity of each one.

> *What is our threshold for e-mail? Survey results from Harris Interactive put the breaking point at fifty e-mails per day.*

A more thoughtful approach to writing effective e-mails, as outlined at the end of this chapter, reduces the load considerably.

## CYA Syndrome

The Gartner Group discovered while investigating e-mail inefficiencies that 30 percent of e-mail is actually "occupational spam," characterized by excessive CC, BCC, and Reply All use. This is what's known as CYA syndrome, or covering your ass.

Just as bad as open loops and blocking, CYA e-mails waste precious time and server space, and are generally unnecessary, despite the sender's intent. "Many people lean toward covering their rears by overinforming their bosses and colleagues," Patricia Wallace, author of *The Internet in the Workplace*, notes. "Then they can say, 'Well, I cc'd you on that debate last month… Didn't you receive it?'"

In response to CYA, managers need to take a stand against overcopying and over-forwarding emails. Alternatives include proactive approaches such as face-to-face discussions if it looks like a controversial situation is in the works, or thoughtful archiving of documentation by the people overseeing the project.

## E-MAIL ACCIDENTS

Hitting Reply All intentionally is one thing. Hitting it accidently can be much, much worse.

In a phone survey in 2009, the Creative Group uncovered some of the most embarrassing Reply All and other sender mistakes made by advertising and marketing executives. Among the worst:

- Sending confidential employee salary information to the whole firm.

- Transmitting confidential client information to another client.

- Sending a copy of an employee's bank records to other employees.

- Sending a job offer to the wrong candidate.

- Sending a résumé to an internal recipient rather than to its intended recipient.

- Sending nasty comments and catty, gossipy e-mails about supervisors directly to those supervisors by mistake.

- Insulting a co-worker and mistakenly copying the entire company.

Some of these examples may sound painfully familiar. The question is, how do you keep yourself from falling into this situation, and what do you do if it happens despite your best efforts?

its subject line). For tips on how to achieve this most effectively, see the next section.

➢ Beyond making your purpose clear and inspiring action, you also want to **leave a good impression** and **make a connection** with the recipient. That means showing some personality while being respectful and polite — and all the while, keeping it short.

---

## THE PSYCHOLOGY OF SENDERS AND RECEIVERS

*A sender's and receiver's goals can be at odds. Senders typically want to show their expertise, their great sense of humor, what a wonderful writer they are, whom they know, what a great product they have, how nice they are, and so on. Too much? In a word, yes.*

*That's why it's so important to put yourself in your recipients' shoes. They have opened your e-mail to find out what it is you want; to get the who, what, when, where, and why without a lot of extra noise. Do they need to read a long exposé on where you met them, what your company history is, every detail of your product or service? Not with the clock ticking and a pile of work in front of them. And if this is a pitch and you're a stranger, your recipient will immediately get defensive.*

> *It's understandable that you want to impress people, make them like you, and be swayed by your vast knowledge, but there are better ways to communicate your needs than with a sprawling document, especially over e-mail. Think about the psychology of your audience, and use it to your best advantage to get what you need from your request.*

## CRAFTING CONCISE E-MAILS

The following tips will help you get the most out of each e-mail you send:

> ➢ **Compose an unambiguous subject line.** Martin Mann of http//:43folders.com has mourned the lost art of subject lines. I couldn't agree more. You have about twenty-five words to get the crux of your idea across in a subject line and ensure your recipient will open the e-mail at all. I would never encourage you to use all twenty-five — ten should be more than plenty. Using action words, followed by a short description, is an effective way to go, for example, "Decision Needed: Logo for new division."

> ➢ **Personalize your e-mails. Don't send blind requests to a large address list.** Impersonalization happens when the "To" list is long and is an immediate road to the

Delete key. Not to mention that it gives everyone on your distribution list access to your address book! **Bcc is a great tool to use to hide your large distribution list.**

➢ **Introduce yourself in a few words.** You wouldn't give your entire bio to someone you just met at a cocktail party; keep it short and sweet in an e-mail as well.

➢ **Be authentic, friendly, and approachable.** Write as you speak rather than in an overly formalized tone, if your corporate climate allows it. Showing a little personality sometimes helps you get a response — just be very careful with jokes or sarcasm that could be misinterpreted.

➢ **State your point upfront.** This can be done with a topic sentence in the first paragraph or a short summary at the top of the page.

➢ **State the action you require clearly,** and if your e-mail requires no action, say so. People will love reading that you require nothing from them. A good mnemonic for this is KISS: "Keep it simple, stupid."

➢ If you *are* calling for a response or action, **clearly state that response's benefits to your recipient.** Don't beat around the bush. People want to know what the point is.

➢ **Don't attach huge files unless they were requested.** It's better to provide a link or offer to send a large file by summarizing what's in it and asking if people want it. Attaching unwanted large files (and most of them are unwanted) simply eats up your recipient's server space. We are not far from the point where documents can be kept "in a cloud" and multiple users can review and comment on their together. SharePoint and Google Docs are already offering this approach to collaboration.

> **Use typographic treatments to simplify your message**. For example, number your points or use bullets to separate them, and put action items in boldface. The easier it is to get the gist of an e-mail at a glance, the better.

> **Use a legible font.** There's nothing worse than an e-mail in ten-point Edwardian Script on a blue checkered background. Stick with a legible size and font, put line spaces between paragraphs, use sentence case (not all caps or all lowercase).

> **Avoid text-message shorthand**. Most companies believe it doesn't have a place in e-mail — shorthand is generally perceived as disrespectful and unprofessional.

> **Don't overuse the "High Importance" marker (that red exclamation mark).** There's a great episode of *The Office* in which Michael Scott is chastised for labeling his e-mails Urgent A, Urgent B, Urgent C, and Urgent D. "Urgent A is the most important.

Urgent D, you don't even really have to worry about," he says. Don't be that guy.

➤ **Write as if your reader is viewing the e-mail on a BlackBerry or smart phone — even if he or she is not.** The less scrolling, the better — without going into shorthand mode.

➤ **Be aware that what you say could be used against you.** Ask yourself the question "If I printed out and taped this message to my boss's door, would I still have a job?"

➤ And finally, **proofread your message, not only for typos, but also for brevity**.

## REPLYING EFFECTIVELY TO OTHERS

Communication is a two-way street, so it's as important to respond effectively to others' e-mails as it is to write effective e-mails yourself.

• **Don't forward long chains.** There's nothing worse than having to slog through pages and pages of information to get to the point you're intended to address. Cut-and-paste the most important information into a new e-mail, or summarize the main points for your new addressee.

• **Be wary of using Reply All.** You know the horror stories. Enough said.

- **Don't copy people simply for the sake of protocol, otherwise known as CYA syndrome.** It's unnecessary, and it's another reason e-mail boxes fill so quickly.

- **Don't carry on open-ended discussions or send "blocking" e-mails.** If your back-and-forth goes on for more than three e-mails without resolution, another form of communication is likely called for. Try picking up the phone.

- **Don't write in anger.** In the end, you'll only suffer for it, with bitter feelings from your colleague or customer, prolonged discussion to remedy the issue, and a bad reputation to boot. A common suggestion I give my clients is to "pause and reflect" before responding to an e-mail that makes them upset. The angrier the e-mail makes you, the longer you should wait before responding.

## Be the Change You Want to See in Cyberspace

Though it can be hard to recognize or admit, we all contribute to the dark side of e-mail with bad e-mail habits. E-mail is an incredibly useful tool, if we use it well. Change begins with you, so start writing the kinds of e-mails you wish to receive. Consistently ask yourself if you're overwriting, being clear, and only copying the essential recipients. Good habits will come back to you — with a more manageable and meaningful inbox.

# CHAPTER 4

# COMMUNICATING ACROSS GENERATIONS

*At work, generational differences can affect everything.*

— GREG HAMMILL,
*"Mixing and Managing Four Generations of Employees"*

Picture this scenario.

A new employee has been hired to a junior position in a large firm. The woman, who is twenty-two, reports to a fifty-something manager who has been working in the industry for more than thirty years, fifteen of them at this particular company.

After less than two months on the job, the younger employee asks to take on some high-level marketing tasks—responsibilities that are outside her position description. She also suggests changing some things: holding fewer meetings (the manager calls at least three a week), increasing flex time so she can get to her rock-climbing gym in the early afternoons, and adding her name to the list of midlevel execs who receive e-mailed weekly sales figures and projections.

Her manager, meanwhile, has made it clear that he thinks meetings are the best way to bring everyone's voice to the table, and he prefers them to her suggested alternative: more IMs and texts, and greater use of the company's project management software. He's spoken to his new employee about the importance of putting work first—and his expectation that she should be logging in at least fifty-five hours a week; he works seventy. Having climbed his way up the corporate ladder from his first job in the mailroom just out of college, he's annoyed that she's asking for high-level tasks and access to privileged information so soon. Plus, he's stunned that he just got an e-mail from her mother requesting that her daughter's ninety-day review be moved up to take place after sixty days, because she knows what a great job Emily's doing for the company and thinks she deserves a raise.

* * *

Welcome to the new work landscape. There are multiple generations working side-by-side, each with a different set of expectations about where work fits into life, the best way to advance, and what level of formality (or informality) should occur at work.

Every single industry is struggling with these changes and how to address its multigenerational challenges. I hear stories about it almost daily.

The reason is pretty clear. For the first time in history, four generations are working together, each with a different background and approach to work and professional relationships.

> *Today, for the first time in history, four generations are working together.*

## WHY FOUR GENERATIONS?

There are lots of reasons for these new workplace demographics.

The economy has definitely played a role, with older workers staying on the job longer to make up for losses to their retirement investments. Industry-specific labor shortages have also caused some employers to recruit or retain employees past age sixty-two. And many people are staying on the job simply because work is so essential to how they define themselves: Baby boomers, who invented the word *workaholic*, are commonly working into their seventies or even longer.

Because competition for talented workers is rising, the workforce is aging—specifically the sixty million people who make up the boomer generation—and people are retiring later in life, old and young will continue to work together in large numbers. In other words, this isn't just a bubble—so we'd better learn how to all get along.

## ORGANIZATIONAL STRUCTURE AND
## GENERATIONAL CHALLENGES

But it's not just demographics that have changed. Organizational structure has changed too.

As I mentioned in chapter 2, most industries now work within a flattened matrix environment instead of inside a traditional vertical hierarchy. Fewer managers oversee a greater number of employees. Participatory management and teamwork are the new normal. So sixty-year-olds may be on equal professional footing with thirty-year-olds, or, in some cases, may even report to them.

One of my clients is experiencing precisely this challenging situation.

Conflict revolves around the older subordinate's perception of respect and desire for autonomy and the younger boss's need for more information and new approaches using new technologies. My involvement has been to help the older employee feel comfortable with those changes; alter his focus so it is on results, not process; and share more information with his boss. Simply getting each of them to understand one another's viewpoints has really moved the relationship forward.

## DEFINING THE FOUR GENERATIONS

When I meet with my clients about generational differences, we start by discussing the historical background of each generation working for the company. This provides a foundation to work from, and frequently provides lively discussion.

Of course, defining generational differences by naming them and classifying them simply by the employees' birth years is not perfect. Depending on which subject matter expert is doing the talking, Veterans might be called the Greatest Generation, Generation Y can be called Millennials, and Baby Boomers might be known as the "me" generation. Birth years for each group aren't set in stone either — and can differ by as much as five years in either direction. That said, the following chart gives some commonly accepted terms and time spans.

| Birth Years | 1922-45 | | 1946-64 | 1965-80 | 1981-2000 |
|---|---|---|---|---|---|
| Generation Name | World War II Veterans Traditionalists | Generation | Baby Boomers | Generation X | Generation Y/ Millennials |

## GENERATIONAL OUTLOOKS

Many studies have explored the values, characteristics, and preferences of generations from veterans to millennials. Though these are generalizations and don't apply to everyone, they are rooted in the values and behaviors associated with specific time periods, such as the Great Depression or the period of civil unrest during the late sixties and early seventies.

Using my seminars and data from a variety of studies, I've created a chart to show some of the traits that most people associate with the various generations, especially as they relate to work.

|  | Veterans | Baby boomers | Generation X | Millennials |
|---|---|---|---|---|
| Traits | Respects Authority Conformist Disciplined | Competitive Optimistic Involved | Skeptical Individualistic Informal | Realistic Confident Social |
| Favored work style | Hard-Working Autonomous | Workaholic Collegial | Independent Pragmatic | Multitasking Egalitarian |
| Favored communication method | One on one Formal memos or letters | Meetings Phone | E-mail One-on-one | Text Social networks |
| Interaction | Individual | Team player | Entrepreneur | Collaborator |
| Messages that motivate | I respect your experience. | The company values you. | Do things your way. | You will work with other bright, creative people. |
| Financial outlook | Pay cash. Save. | Buy now, pay later. | Be cautious. Save. | Earn it, spend it. |

## HISTORICAL BASIS FOR GENERATIONAL OUTLOOKS

Being born in a certain year doesn't automatically mean you're assigned these traits, of course. But historical events do shape us. Let take a brief look at some of the events whose impact resonates with these four generations:

- The Great Depression and World War II created a preference for **"command-and-control" leadership** among members of the **veteran generation.** They make decisions based on what has worked in the past, and tend toward a formal and disciplined work style. They are loyal, thorough, and hard-working.

- **Baby boomers** prefer a more **collegial work style**, reflecting their experiences with cultural movements such as the civil rights era, the women's movement, and antiwar protests during Vietnam. But interestingly enough, they are also competitive — most likely because of their generation's large size. Boomers **equate work with self-worth**, and were the first **workaholics**. They tend to like **teamwork** and **group decision making**.

- **Gen Xers** are **independent** because many of them grew up as latchkey kids — their parents were those workaholic boomers. They also saw the breakdown of a lot of institutions — marriage, government, business — so gen Xers tend to be skeptical and trust only themselves. Having lived through the computer revolution, they are **computer-savvy**, but they're also **pragmatic** and **like direct communication**. **Work–life balance** is very important to them.

- **Millennials** were **shaped by technology**. They are very close to their parents and thus see relationships with other generations as much more **egalitarian** than their predecessors do. They often have a casual approach to life in the way they dress, communicate, and generally present themselves. Millennials are **multitaskers, value teamwork, embrace diversity**, and are **adaptable to change**.

---

## THE LOST GENERATION

*The "lost generation" represents a subset of the Millennial generation that has been saddled with a name all its own, the result of graduating from college right around the time of the Great Recession of 2008.*

*This unfortunate group of graduates sought to enter the workforce during an extremely difficult period — when most companies were laying people off, not hiring. If jobs were available in a particular industry, they typically went to people with experience rather than those fresh out of school, leaving the lost generation struggling to establish their careers. Once the economy began improving, a new slate of millennial graduates snapped up any junior positions to be found, leaving the lost generation out in the cold.*

---

## GENERATIONAL MYTHS

While there is clearly some accuracy as to how members of each generation perform and interact at work, there are also some common misconceptions.

The inaccuracy I most commonly have to confront regards millennials. Because this group works to live — unlike the Baby Boomers, who live to work — they are often perceived by their bosses (usually boomers) as wanting opportunities to be handed to them. Millennials are more interested in making work a component of life, not its center, but that doesn't mean they aren't driven. In fact, a major survey has shown that millennials are very self-reliant and entrepreneurial. Their sense of egalitarianism can make them appear overly aggressive to those accustomed to a more traditional, hierarchical approach. But I don't think it's such a bad thing to advocate for oneself at work, especially if it comes from a place of wanting to learn and grow.

Similarly, gen Xers are sometimes perceived as unwilling to work hard, baby boomers are chided as being the selfish "Me" generation, and veterans may be disregarded as employees just biding time until they can retire. In all three cases, research has proven these stereotypes to by and large be untrue. To discover what background and experiences a particular person is drawing from, it's important to set aside preconceived notions, to pay attention to who that person is as an individuals, and to focus on productivity, metrics, and results rather than work style and birth year.

## EACH GENERATION SPEAKS A
## DIFFERENT WORK LANGUAGE

Communication can be one of the biggest hurdles workers face when interacting across generations. As the "generational communications" chart shows, different age groups have competing preferences for how they communicate and what communication style is the most effective for others when interacting with them: for example, being formal versus informal, interacting face to face versus with a text message, e-mail, or IM, or discussing project goals in a group setting versus one on one. Some workers see certain communication styles as efficient and others as burdensome, while other workers view those same styles as lacking good business etiquette or simply the only way to conduct themselves professionally.

In their *2008 Technology Gap Survey*, LexisNexis explored the legal profession in an effort to better understand how different generations use technology to communicate. The results were fascinating and can probably be applied to almost every other profession:

- 77 percent of boomers surveyed agree that PDAs and mobile phones contribute to a decline in proper workplace etiquette and believe the use of a laptop during in-person meetings is "distracting." Only 44 percent of millennial legal professionals agree.

- Only 23 percent of boomers surveyed believe using laptops or PDAs during in-person meetings is "efficient." Nearly half of millennial legal professionals think it is.

- 27 percent of boomer legal professionals think blogging about work-related issues is acceptable, compared with 52 percent of millennial legal professionals.

So where do all these discrepancies leave us?

## THE TITANIUM RULE

The most important thing to keep in mind when working with other generations is not the Golden Rule, but the Titanium Rule: Do unto others, keeping their preferences in mind.

That means being aware of all these different work and communication styles, understanding other perspectives, and, when it's appropriate, adjusting your own style to make your interaction more productive.

In other words, put results ahead of process.

During my multigenerational training programs, this is the time where many managers have their "aha moment" and realize they may have been more closed off to new ideas than they thought. My goal is to help them figure out ways to remain open and flexible and focused on results when they go back to the office.

A client I talked to recently put the Titanium Rule to work in his office, and this was his reaction: "I just made a few adjustments and a few comments to show that I understood where the other person was coming from, and it made the whole interaction go so much more smoothly. Had I not gone Titanium, I was headed straight for our usual contentious interaction."

You don't have to abandon who you are or how you like to work to do this. You just need to put yourself in your colleague's shoes. The biggest change will be how you approach the situation with your colleagues. Keeping their point of view in mind and understanding their perspective can make a significant impact on how the interaction progresses.

## TOOLS AND TECHNIQUES FOR COMMUNICATING ACROSS GENERATIONS IN THE WORKPLACE

The challenges of a workplace that includes four generations spanning forty or even fifty years may seem insurmountable, but they're really not. The biggest step is getting to know each colleague's outlook. You can't understand it until you spend some time considering his or her background, influences, and motivations at work. Here are some basic strategies for taking into account generational differences:

> ➤ **Be aware of the generations represented in your organization**. What percentage are veterans, boomers, gen Xers, and millennials? Think about where you fall in this mix.

Some companies perform a formal audit of their staff as a starting point to determine the extent they need to focus on the issues related to generational differences.

➤ **Initiate conversation about the differences between the generations**. This could be handled through the company's human resources department. Not only will this conversation help people understand one another and avoid judging them, it can also be a lot of fun.

➤ **Keep those generational outlooks in mind as you interact with others in your company.** One of the first steps toward working well with others and establishing a more productive and comfortable work environment may be simply to understand the background, motives, and work style of your co-worker's generation.

➤ **Ask people how they prefer to communicate.** Just as you set your own communication style, so do others. Asking and abiding by other people's preferences will make them feel respected and will make them want to work more effectively with you. Compromise can be essential.

➤ **In addition to asking, make it a point to learn more about the interactive styles of each generation you work with, and adjust how you communicate with them**

**accordingly.** AARP's report *Leading a Multigenerational Workforce* is a great source of information, as is *Generational Differences in the Workplace,* a University of Minnesota report by Anick Tolbize. Some observations and suggestions for communicating well with other generations based on the studies cited in those publications include:

| WWII Generation/Veterans | Baby Boomers |
|---|---|
| • Respectful tone<br>• No slang or profanity<br>• Professional language | • Conversational tone<br>• Invite participation<br>• Relate to individual vision |

| Generation X | Millennials |
|---|---|
| • Direct language<br>• Avoid corporate speak<br>• Use email or voice mail | • Positive language<br>• Relate to personal goals<br>• Use text message or informally meet face to face |

➢ **Be aware of how others perceive your technology etiquette**, and be polite in how you use your phone, and computer, and other devices. This doesn't mean you have to stop using your PDA or smart phone in front of others, but you may wish to preface your actions with a statement like "Excuse me, but I am waiting for an important e-mail from a client, and I need to check this."

➢ **When working on a team project with different generations, decide how you plan to communicate from the beginning.** Millenials prefer to communicate using the latest technology, Boomers tend to prefer face to face and Xers like email so establishing guidelines as to how updates and information will be shared will help prevent miscommunication.

➢ **Pursue different perspectives.** Value others' opinions — even when they differ from your own. A diverse workplace offers many advantages, including flexibility, innovation, creativity, and the ability to relate to an intergenerational marketplace.

> *A diverse workplace offers many advantages, including flexibility, innovation, creativity, and the ability to relate to an intergenerational marketplace.*

➢ **Establish mentorship programs to help broaden people's understanding and respect for one another.** Working closely with another and learning from his or her experience can build great respect and build a valuable relationship. Keep in mind that younger generations can mentor older generations as well as the reverse: For example, veterans and boomers can gain a great deal from the technological savvy of younger peers, while the older generations can use their experience and institutional knowledge to help the younger.

➢ **Take special care with millennials.** Bringing the youngest generation of co-workers into the fold presents special challenges. As they move into the workforce in large numbers, it's important to understand their work and communication styles. The *Harvard Business Review* offers these suggestions to managers supervising these younger workers:

- Spend three minutes explaining tasks to millennials to get them excited, help them see the benefits, and allow them to gain insight into the decision-making process.

- Give millennials some decision-making authority; don't let them fall into "learned helplessness."

- Invite interaction.

- Set short-term projects for the highest productivity.

- Be genuine and not overly authoritative.

## BENEFITS OF A MULTIGENERATIONAL WORKFORCE

Despite their differences, veterans, boomers, gen Xers, and millennials have a lot of things in common, especially in expectations from work. All workers can agree they want work to:

- Provide personal fulfillment and satisfaction.
- Make them feel valued.
- Provide a supportive environment.
- Offer career development.
- Provide flexibility.

These shared goals can be common ground for recognizing differences among the generations in today's workforce, and finding ways to make those differences strengths.

# CHAPTER 5

# THE VIRTUAL WORKER CHALLENGE

*A virtual team is more than the sum of its members — it's a culture with a life of its own.*

— HTTP://WWW.CEOCONSULTANT.COM,
*"7 Steps to Exceptional Virtual Team Communication"*

It wasn't long ago that the notion of working virtually seemed like a plot twist for the Sci-Fi channel. Yet here we are, not very deep into the twenty-first century, and millions of people are working from home, in a satellite office, at a local coffee shop, or from pretty much any location they choose, thanks to the modern miracle of high-speed Internet connections, laptop computers, and handheld devices.

The combination of portable hardware and fast, highly accessible broadband capacity has truly revolutionized where and when people work. Just take a look at these numbers, which quantify this decade's dramatic workplace transformation:

| | 2005 | 2006 | 2008 |
|---|---|---|---|
| Employee plus contract workers telecommuting one day or more per month | 26.1 million | 28.7 million | 33.7 million |
| Percentage increase over previous figure | .05 percent | 1 percent | 17 percent |

Data source: *Telework Trendlines 2009*, WorldatWork, http:// www.workingfromanywhere.com.

In the coming decades, it seems likely that the virtual work environment trend will continue. And with this change from office space in cyberspace will come both vast improvements in communication and productivity and obstacles and unanticipated bumps in the road.

## WHAT IS VIRTUAL WORK?

Before we get started in discussing pros and cons, I'd like to take a moment to define working virtually. Because it's still pretty new to our vocabulary, virtual work has lots of other names too. It's also called telecommuting, teleworking, e-lancing, remote working, mobile working, and workshifting.

No matter what the terminology, virtual work is defined as:

- Using an Internet connection to work remotely one or more days per month
  - at home
  - at a client's office
  - at a satellite office
  - at another location (restaurant, hotel, airplane, library, etc.)
- And/or using technology to conduct meetings with people in a variety of locations

Forrester Consulting did a survey in 2010 to determine where people work in a typical week. It's interesting to see by how great a margin people have shifted away from the office environment. "Company headquarters" still made the top of the list, but by a pretty slim margin: 62 percent. Other locations named were "home" (23 percent), "a satellite office" (20 percent), "client site" (11 percent), "while traveling" (11 percent), and "other" (6 percent). Eighteen percent of U.S. information workers reported working from several locations; the same was true for 36 percent of European information workers.

Both employers and workers are propelling this trend forward at a steady clip. Employers make virtual work possible by offering their staff more flex time, hiring people from a variety of locations to make up a single work team, establishing satellite offices or telework centers, and acquiring the technology to make it happen—from remote desktop capability to Web and video conferencing to collaborative workspaces. In addition, employees are stepping up to ask if they can do at least part of their work away from the office, and are eagerly embracing the technology to make it happen. In fact, a recent poll by the nonprofit WorldatWork showed that of those people not currently telecommuting, 50 percent were either very interested or interested in doing some of their work virtually.

## The Advantages of Virtual Work

Why the big rush away from the office? For most employees, telecommuting has many perks. Workers can avoid bumper-to-bumper traffic, not have to worry about shoveling the driveway or navigating through fog, ice, or rain, work in a quiet, comfortable setting, keep themselves at arm's length from company politics and gossip, and perhaps most appealing, better balance their home and work lives. This last perk is especially attractive to generation X and millennial workers who, as we learned in the last chapter, would rather not spend every waking moment at their desks.

And come to find out, much of the work people do doesn't hinge on being at a company location. Thirty-eight percent of people polled think they could do some portion of their work remotely. Of that 38 percent, nearly three quarters think they could do between 20 percent and 80 percent of their work away from the office, as this pie chart illustrates:

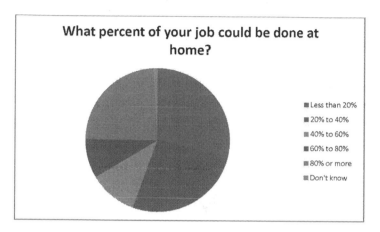

**What percent of your job could be done at home?**

- Less than 20%
- 20% to 40%
- 40% to 60%
- 60% to 80%
- 80% or more
- Don't know

Note: Percentages are based on weighted data, while sample sizes shown ("n") reflect the actual number of respondents. Data source: *Telework Trendlines February 2009 Survey,* WorldatWork, http://www.workingfromanywhere.org.

For employers, the advantages are just as compelling—and speak directly to the bottom line. Some of the incentives include:

- Lower overhead and travel expenses.
- Improved productivity.
- A low- or no-cost benefit to employees.
- The ability to identify and engage talent from around the world.
- The opportunity to take advantage of multicultural viewpoints.

- The ability to respond to the challenges of the global marketplace.

Companies that have made the switch are seeing some pretty impressive savings. Telework Research Network reported in 2010 that Best Buy's average productivity increased 35 percent after it instituted increased telecommuting among its workers. British Telecom saw a 20 percent increase. And Dow Chemical estimates that the company benefitted with a $32.5 million increase in productivity thanks to incorporating a virtual work atmosphere.

## WHOSE TIME IS IT?

So it seems like virtual work is a win-win situation for all. But there are definitely some challenges to out-of-office work.

The question of when the work day ends is a huge one. Just one example: Results from a survey conducted by Cohesive Knowledge Solutions, a company established to help people more efficiently manage their e-mail, show that the average professional spends fifty minutes a day sending e-mails after work. (This survey took place in 2008, so the numbers have probably increased since that time.) So, if all your work is available in your home or wherever you may be, are you obligated to deal with office issues 24/7?

Lawsuits have been filed based on that very question. Hourly employees who feel their employers expect them to answer e-mail and phone calls no matter what the time, especially when their cell phone, smart phone, or PDA was provided by the company, are asking why they're not being paid overtime to work when they're technically off the clock. On http://msnbc.com, Joseph Pisani writes that "lawyers are advising their corporate clients to update their policies and handbooks related to BlackBerry use and reconsider who gets a device."

## MANAGEMENT CONSIDERATIONS

On the other side of the coin, there are some employees who just aren't as productive in a non-company environment as they are in the office. I've worked with people who are really good, hard workers, but if they work one day a week in a virtual atmosphere, they see it as a day off. They may be checking in and responding to e-mails, but they aren't initiating work and are certainly not as productive as they would be in the office. In cases like these, the onus is on the manager to make sure those who have the benefit of telecommuting are being responsible, and that their productivity goals are clear. Companies approach this in a variety of ways: by monitoring login and logout times, watching activity on remote desktops, and making sure e-mails are being replied to in a timely fashion.

There can definitely be some resentment among in-office workers that telecommuters are getting a better deal. At one company I consulted for, there was a perception among the administrative and warehouse staff that workers given the privilege of telecommuting were slacking off. A cartoon anonymously appeared in the break room picturing a person wearing pajamas in bed with the TV on, a phone to her ear, and a box of pizza next to her with the caption "Working from Home." It didn't win any points with part-time virtual workers, who were in fact very productive during their out-of-office time. The misconception that virtual work means free time must be addressed so that productivity is not compromised.

## VIRTUAL COMMUNICATION TOOLS

There are numerous tools that can be implemented to make virtual workers more productive and accountable.

The tools that work best for various industries depend on individual and company needs — and on budgetary constraints and training requirements. A 2010 survey done by Forrester Research took a look at what new communication tools companies had or were adding in order to make virtual work more effective. Not surprisingly, e-mail came first; I'd be surprised to hear of a modern company that has not yet introduced electronic communication.

When asked "What collaboration technologies does your firm utilize?" Here are the results among the 921 respondents.

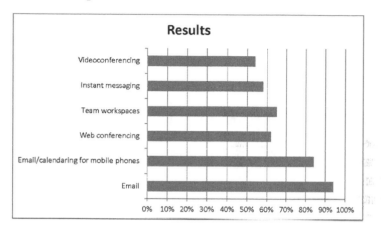

Source: *Enterprise and SMB Software Survey,* North America and Europe, 2009.

But as we've already explored, e-mail has its limitations. According to OSHA, studies show that approximately 83 percent of human learning occurs visually, with two or more people interacting face to face. Audio conferencing, which has also been in use for years, obviously lacks a visual component too, and so is most effective when there are extra verbal check-ins to make sure the participants are understanding what is being communicated. The lack of visual cues is where virtual work limited to e-mail and phone calls can fall down, as I'll explore further below. As a result, I recommend that firms consider videoconferencing and additional in-person meetings as much as they possibly can. There is a much better chance of engagement when you can physically see someone.

In addition to budget and training, privacy issues can also restrict the types of technology various companies are able to adopt. I recently conducted a large program for a firm where client confidentiality was a major concern. Though the client needed to introduce technology to enhance the virtual work experience, there was also a need to be mindful of to the security of client information. Retailers, banks, and credit card processors and of course the health care industry have all dealt with client privacy issues in recent years, so it's a very important issue for companies to address when there is a large contingency of virtual workers.

## TEAM BUILDING

Two hurdles to effectively build team environment in the virtual workspace include finding the best technology and tools and achieving balanced productivity — not expecting too much and not accepting too little from team members.

In any form of communication where people aren't able to observe body language, see facial expressions, or pick up on other visual cues — e-mail, audio conferencing, discussion forums, collaboration workspaces — it can be difficult to establish camaraderie and trust among members of a team. That lack of connectedness can turn into misunderstanding when tone, body language, and facial expression aren't there to help people better read a situation, as we explored in chapter 3. Add to that age and cultural differences that exist when employees are coming together from vastly different backgrounds and cultures, and you can end up with some pretty uncomfortable situations.

Good virtual etiquette is thus part of team building. How many of us have been in a conference call with others only to hear someone tapping on his or her computer in the background? Or how about when you ask a participant a question and he or she hasn't the slightest clue of what's been discussed so far? It's just as important to be alert and focused in a virtual meeting as it is during an in-person one.

## PERFORMANCE REVIEWS

Virtual workers still need very real feedback and performance reviews. Establishing the appropriate rapport over an Internet or phone connection during performance reviews can present significant challenges.

Based on my consulting experience, performance reviews of virtual employees can at times be ineffective and counterproductive for both the boss and the employee.

The most common question I hear from managers when discussing this issue is "How do I give a performance review via phone and make sure that I am conveying exactly what I want to convey and at the same time get a sense of how the employee is taking what I am telling them?" My tried-and-true solution is for supervisors to *overcommunicate* in the way they speak to their employees and the way they listen since there are no nonverbal cues to keep everyone on the same page. That means checking in constantly with comments and questions such as "Tell me your thoughts so far." "Please tell me your concerns." "Do you agree?" "Can you elaborate?"

The same techniques are useful in any nonvisual meeting, not just performance reviews. But it's not solely the manager's responsibility to make sure good communication is happening. Employees also have to overcommunicate and should step up and clarify any confusion or conflict that arises. Optimal communication is bidirectional and involves give and take from the manager and employee.

## TOOLS AND TECHNIQUES FOR IMPROVING VIRTUAL COMMUNICATION

Whether it's finding ways to balance work and leisure time when your office is literally anywhere, managing technology effectively, or building better teams and using better online etiquette, there are lots of ways to make virtual tools work in your favor.

## BALANCING WORK AND LIFE

Many of the tips given in chapter 2 for managing the nonstop flow of information during your off time apply to virtual work as well:

> If your telecommuting generally takes place from home, use a **separate physical space** to do your work as much as possible. Rather than making the run of the house your office space, set aside a room or a physically defined section of a room as your workspace, and try not to use it for other purposes.

> **Stick to a schedule**. Don't automatically jump on to your work computer or PDA and check e-mail during evenings and weekends. Learn to set time boundaries for yourself regarding when you work and when you don't. Since everyone in my family has a smart phone or BlackBerry, I insist on technology-free times so we can shut out the outside world for a while and just enjoy family time.

> **Turn off your handheld device or computer** during non-work hours. If you have a traditional office and your company allows it (for legal purposes, they may even encourage this), leave your work device at work.

> **Let colleagues know that you won't be available after a certain (reasonable) time.** To make the case to your boss, you might let him or her know that not being connected 24/7 will increase your productivity during regular work hours—whatever the two of you have agreed "regular" is.

## TECHNOLOGY CHALLENGES

> **Use technology appropriate to your work and work style**. Though this depends on what your company offers, keep in mind what tasks work best for a conference call (typically passive delivery of information), in a meeting or videoconference (more active, participatory brainstorming), via e-mail (targeted requests for information, inquiries, or action), and so on.

> **If you are looking to enhance the technology your team uses, assign one person as the technology guru** to investigate the tools that will work best for your team, telecommuters in your department, or telecommuters throughout the company. Millennials can be a good bet for doing this sort of research if members of your IT team are not available.

> **Once you have a sense of what might work best for you and have had time to demo free downloads, discuss with your boss and team the virtues of different virtual communication tools.** For example, Web conferencing can include virtual rooms, whiteboard functions, voting tools, cameras, and informal chat rooms for side discussions.

> **Test the technology you choose and always have backup plan**. There's nothing worse than starting a meeting and running into problems midway.

➤ **Train others in how to use the technology**. If you are forming a team that will work virtually, meeting with a client online, or helping a new employee in your department get onboard the virtual work train, it's helpful to show them the ropes.

## TEAM BUILDING AND GOOD VIRTUAL ETIQUETTE

➤ Even when people can't see you, **it's important to be focused on interactions with others when you are working virtually;** for example, don't mute your phone when you are a part of an audioconference and don't multitask during a videoconference by e-mailing, texting, and so on. **The manners that apply in person apply virtually as well.**

➤ Though you may only interact with certain colleagues online, it's important to **connect with them on a personal level**. Don't overdo this by sending e-mail jokes or overly chatty messages (see chapter 3), but be sure you create business relationships with some personal warmth.

➤ **When working with a full-time virtual team, meet in person or use Skype or some other sort of visual tool as often as possible.**

In-person meetings may only happen once a year or quarter, but they are vital to creating a goal-oriented team approach. Skype and other forms of video conferencing are a nice alternative to a purely computer-to-computer relationship with other team members.

➤ **When working with people from other countries, learn their cultural differences in work style**. Chapter 6 speaks to this issue more fully, but a good place to start is the website http://www.worldbusinessculture.com.

➤ **Alternate the times of meetings you hold with colleagues in other parts of the country or world** so you don't always inconvenience the same people. That small concession on everyone's part will make the team stronger as a whole.

➤ **Virtual teams must work as effectively as in-person teams do**. Whether you manage teams that work virtually or are a member of them, build a team with strong leadership, aligned goals, respect for diversity, and complementary working styles.

➤ **If you don't fully understand an issue or feel part of a discussion, speak up.** When you don't share a room with the people you work with, there may be a feeling of being disconnected. Overcommunicating is essential when the main form of interaction you have with people is through e-mail or on the phone. The same is true during performance evaluations. Clarify, elaborate, and state your concerns.

## THE FUTURE OF VIRTUAL WORK

There's little doubt that the virtual workforce will continue to grow as technology expands and workers and employers take advantage of the many benefits of telecommuting. Working virtually could be one of the major societal shifts of our time, allowing people to live almost anywhere, minimize the stress and inefficiencies of commuting, and to have more time and energy to connect with their families, friends, and loved ones — but only if we put into place the appropriate tools, rules, and training.

# CHAPTER 6

# GLOBALIZATION

*Whether someone is looking for a new supplier, giving a presentation, or negotiating a contract, intercultural communication can, does, and will play an important role. It impacts our ability to communicate effectively within a culture as well as how we are perceived.*

— KWINTESSENTIAL.CO.UK

As I'm sure you've noticed, the world is getting smaller and smaller—maybe not literally, but definitely virtually. In the last thirty years especially, globalization has had the effect of breaking down international boundaries. We now live on a planet with a multinational economy and a global marketplace, where your customers could be in Europe, your suppliers in China, your workforce in India, and your headquarters in the United States. Or almost any other combination—take your pick.

What's made this possible? Political changes, generational changes, and technology have all contributed. But the introduction of new channels of communication has been the predominant force in facilitating global communication. The Internet, cloud computing, social networking, and automation have accelerated our ability to reach each other, trade with one another, invest in countries outside our own, share data, outsource labor, transport goods more efficiently, and transmit vital information instantaneously.

As just one example, a company I consult for works in over 100 countries around the world. In addition to expanding their business opportunities, globalization is a key recruiting point for potential employees. Employees of this company obtain exposure to multiple cultures and varied environments, and often have the potential for travel and relocation. For recruitment of young workers especially (think Millennials), this social and global experience can be a huge draw.

## THE NUMBERS

We all hear about globalization in the news, and when you take a look at the numbers, it really hits home how much globalization has changed the way companies operate:

- Eighty percent of U.S. products were competing in international markets by the end of the twentieth century.

Just look in your refrigerator, on your shelves, or in your driveway to see evidence of globalization.

Due to the ease of international transport and communications, products once associated with a particular country can now be made pretty much anywhere. That Grey Poupon mustard in your fridge is not manufactured in France, it's made in the United States. Toyota trucks are built in Texas, not Japan, and your Ford could be from Mexico instead of Detroit. The same is true for almost any product. So how does globalization affect all the people involved in our economy, from manufacturing to finance to the service industry, technology, and everything in between?

## BEING NIMBLE IN A GLOBALIZED WORLD

In a word, this ever-shrinking world is making it imperative that workers become nimble.

The good news is that the skills that serve people well in the United States usually serve them well in other places too. According to the National Association of Colleges and Employers Job Outlook 2011 survey, the skills that were found most attractive to prospective employers were ranked as:

1. Verbal communication skills
2. Strong work ethic
3. Teamwork skills
4. Analytical skills
5. Initiative

What changes on a worldwide stage in relation to these skills?

## IT'S NOT JUST THE LANGUAGE

It starts with communication. But there's a lot more to working with international markets than just learning a new language. Nonverbal cues can be even more important to some cultures than the words that are chosen. I find it amazing how cultural norms can vary from one culture to the next. Local customs can govern how to greet people, rules of conducting a meeting, methods of voicing disagreement, and even how to appropriately dress, eat, and relax with others.

A few examples:

- In China, looking down is considered a sign of respect.

- In Korea, it's considered rude to say no.

- In Mexico, arriving on time or early for a meal shows bad manners.

- In Britain, asking someone what part of the country they come from is viewed as trying to determine their class, and is inappropriate.

- In India, you should give and receive business cards only with your right hand.

These expressions of culture are just the tip of the iceberg. Beneath them lie deeply ingrained beliefs about how to indicate respect, the importance of hierarchy, how men and women should be treated, or whether the group's importance supersedes the individual's—just to name a few.

## CULTURAL DIFFERENCES

Communicating across international lines can be complicated, but no matter who you are working with, getting a grip on the business environment you're entering follows a straightforward step-by-step process. First, learn about the people. Then, learn about the way they do business. Finally, learn about the corporate culture of the specific company you are working with, especially in terms of how it fits into the overarching culture.

There are great resources available to guide you across these cultural gaps. RW3's Culture Wizard at http://rw-3.com is one. It offers questionnaires to help you establish cultural profiles for everyone on your team, including yourself; detailed information on the cultural styles of a wide variety of nationalities; tools to help you work more effectively with people across the globe; and lots of other good information. Kwintessential.co.uk and world-businessculture.com also offer guides to customs and etiquette for dozens of countries. Business consultant and Professor Sana Reynolds' book *Guide to Cross-Cultural Communication* (Prentice Hall, 2010) can also be helpful in finding materials and helping to navigate new territory.

Based on those resources and my own experience, here are some essential strategies you need to consider when interacting with another culture.

- What is the culture's **structure**? Is it hierarchical or egalitarian? Can decisions be made only by the person at the top are they made in a group setting?

- How **formal or casual** is the culture? What is the most appropriate way to introduce yourself, interact in a meeting, present a business plan, eat a meal, tell a joke, or say goodbye?

- Do people **communicate directly or indirectly**? Is saying no outright considered rude? Do you need to give permission to others to end a phone call? Or is it better to state things upfront?

- Is **time** looked upon as fluid or structured? This can affect such things as the length and organization of a meeting, how deadlines are interpreted, and whether it is best to be punctual or slightly late.

- What are the roles of **politics** and **religion** in the business culture of the country? What are the expectations of foreigners so they don't disrespect long-held beliefs?

- How about **family relationships**? Do you need to inquire about your colleague's spouse and children before each interaction, bring pictures of your own family to share, or extend invitations to your home or visit others'?

- What's the **dynamic between men and women**? Do women have a place in the business world? If so, are they treated in a different manner? Should women dress, speak, or interact in a specific way?

- Does this culture value **gift giving**? If it does, what is an appropriate or, more importantly, inappropriate gift? Should it be opened in front of the giver?

- Are there religious or national **holidays** that affect business, such as Chinese New Year or Ramadan?

- And how about all those small interactions that show you understand and respect another culture? Should you **maintain eye contact** or **look down**, **speak softly** out of respect or **raise your voice** to show interest, **shake hands** or **bow**, **sit quietly** or **interrupt** during a conversation?

As you can see, navigating cultural differences can be complicated, but doing so is integral to global success. And not only is it important to learn about others' culture, it's equally crucial not to ignore your own culture and customs.

## AN EXAMPLE

One of my clients discovered the complexities of working cross-culturally when ordering samples from a vendor in China.

What seemed like a simple task quickly became complicated. The client e-mailed the vendor in her usual friendly way that she needed three material samples by Thursday. No one responded to the e-mail until the following Tuesday. Then the message came back from the male vendor: "Received your request. Two samples will be delivered next Thursday." One week late and one sample short. And the client's boss was getting impatient. What was going on?

First, my client needed to think about her own culture. Americans tend to function at a very quick pace. They belong to what's called a "controlled time" culture. Deadlines are the name of the game, workdays are long and breaks are short, and there's always a sense of needing to have things done yesterday. Americans are also informal and egalitarian. They don't give much thought to their casual communication style and easy interaction across gender lines. It's hard to remember that the whole world doesn't work this way.

Then my client needed to think about the vendor's culture. China functions in what's called "moderate time," where there is some flexibility to schedules and deadlines. They also have a very hierarchical and formal structure, where certain rules of etiquette must be followed. Gender bias also exists in China, especially in a business setting. They, too, are taken aback when others don't function this way.

So there were several components at play that made this interaction less than successful.

First, the vendor probably didn't see a problem with missing the exact time frames given to her by her American customer. Even so, that more fluid view of time is changing now that China has become such a force in global manufacturing. So for my client, straightening things out might simply involve reinforcing to the vendor the importance of deadlines and how missing them could have downstream effects on the rest of her company.

Next is the issue of formality. The client would probably have gotten better results if she'd used a more formal tone in her e-mail and established herself as the final authority in making decisions. Gender bias may have been in play as well, even though the Chinese vendor was also a woman. So, though it's an unusual situation for an American woman, having her older, male boss establish her authority could have been helpful.

The abruptness of the e-mail also bothered my client. What she didn't know is that Chinese tend to go directly to the subject at hand in written communication, and they still don't see e-mail as an official form of communication. So an initial or follow-up phone call would have helped, as well as setting the expectation that e-mails would be short and to the point.

## DIALOGIC MODEL OF COMMUNICATION

As you can see by the last example, it's important to once again apply the Titanium Rule and to keep others' preferences in mind when working cross-culturally, just as when working cross-generationally. In *Strategic Management Communication for Leaders*, Robyn Walker defines this communication style as the dialogic method of communication. She writes, "The strategies that we use to communicate must take into account how our messages affect others' perception of us as well as the effect of our communication on others. This [dialogic] model implicitly recognizes the growing importance of interpersonal relationships upon our own success and happiness in the workplace."

According to Walker, the dialogic model has developed over time from three other types of communication: information transfer, transactional process, and strategic control. Here are her definitions of all four styles:

- **Communication as Information Transfer** assumes that everyone can clearly convey his or her thoughts to another person without confusion or distortion of information.

- **Communication as Transactional Process** sees the sender and receiver of information as active participants in conveying information, but still assumes that shared meaning is clear.

- **Communication as Strategic Control** is a style where individuals use communication to control their environment, without great concern for the receiver's social, political, or ethical views.

- **Communication as Dialogue Process** is where the receiver's perspective must be considered in order for interpretation of the message to be clear.

It's pretty clear, based on the vast differences in the way various cultures interact, why the last model would be the most effective. Walker points out the need for communicators to trust, respect, and accept one another despite their differences. I couldn't agree more.

## Tools and Techniques for Improving Cross-Cultural Communication

Here are some tips to make cross-cultural communication easier. These are just a starting point. I urge you to investigate the culture you are doing business with carefully to learn more about how they work and how you can best work with them.

➢ Be **self-aware**. One of the first steps in communicating effectively with others is understanding how you communicate and what your cultural norms are. Generally,

Americans are seen as individualistic, informal, and direct—sometimes to the point of rudeness. How do you interact with others? What cultural traditions are part of your makeup?

➤ Have an **open mind**. It's human nature to see your own culture as superior and other ways of interaction as strange or ineffective. Try to eliminate your internal biases and our tendency toward ethnocentricity. Put yourself in others' shoes, and be respectful of differences rather than being critical of them. Hopefully they will return the favor.

➤ Be **patient**. In cultures where building relationships and closely observing hierarchy are important, such as India, China, or Saudi Arabia, Americans may be frustrated by what they perceive as long, micromanaged meetings. It's important to recognize differences in the way people do business and accommodate and appreciate those differences.

➤ Be **inquisitive**. Other cultures are fascinating. Learn as much as you can about the culture you are doing business with by **researching, reading, taking intercultural courses, talking to colleagues** who know the culture in question, and simply **watching** and **listening**. Online resources are a good start; try http://rw-3.com, www.qwintessential. co.uk, or http://www.worldbusinessculture. com for some good information on cultural styles. It's interesting to read about your own culture, too.

➤ **Listen actively and summarize points to make sure they are clear.** Language barriers as well as cultural differences can cause confusion over meaning. Be sure you are not missing any subtleties in a conversation by being thorough as you interact.

➤ **Be careful with jokes.** Americans tend to use humor to make people comfortable, but it doesn't always translate well to other cultures. In many countries—for example, China—business is viewed as a very serious endeavor, and humor rarely has a place at the table.

➤ If you don't know the language, **learn basic phrases** and use them to show respect. Just saying hello, thank you, pleased to meet you, and so on can go a long way.

➤ **Mimic the body language of your hosts**. If direct eye contact, placing your hands on the table, or using a vice grip in a handshake are not culturally appropriate, follow the lead of the people around you.

➤ When speaking to international colleagues, don't use **American jargon**, be sure to **speak slowly**, and **avoid raising your voice** when you are not understood. We are often not cognizant of how quickly or loudly we're speaking, and it's something to be aware of. Also, make sure you **interact with the**

**person speaking rather than the translator** when a translator is involved.

> **If you make a mistake, apologize**. It's important to show that you see your error and are not purposefully being rude.

---

## BRAVE NEW WORLD

International communication is challenging, but it can be rewarding and is often vital to success in today's business world. Don't let cultural barriers keep you from forming strong business relationships. As you work cross-culturally, keep the interests of your international colleagues on the same level of importance as your organization's interests, and you'll find your interactions to be much more enjoyable and worthwhile.

# CHAPTER 7

# THE FUTURE OF COMMUNICATION

*Communication works for those who work at it.*

—JOHN POWELL

As we've explored in the last six chapters, the previous decade has brought enormous changes to communication in the workplace. E-mail and the Internet have overloaded us with information. A multigenerational workforce has challenged us to understand one another, despite age and varying backgrounds. Virtual tools have taken us out of the office and blurred the lines between work and free time. And globalization has brought together cultures like never before. It's my hope that this book has given you the tools and techniques you need to help you better manage these challenges, embrace the opportunities they offer, and to provide crucial communication strategies for the modern workplace.

There's one more question I'd like to consider: What lies ahead? If there's anything we can count on, it's sure to involve change.

## PREDICTIONS

The future is hard to predict, but studying the past and the present can provide us with clues. There are major trends we can assume will continue: The influence of collaborative teams and virtual workers. An increasingly globalized workforce. Expanded use of electronic communication. So what will the workplace look like going forward?

## WORKSPACES

It is likely that physical office space will evolve to accommodate new communication advances. In my work in corporate environments, I'm already seeing this evolution start to occur. Large rooms containing rows of desks with no dividers in between and multiple shared meeting spaces are replacing the traditional setup of cubicles, a single conference room, and private managerial offices. Some companies, as I mentioned earlier, don't even have assigned desks. People just sit down and plug in depending on their day's assignment or their team's needs.

Younger generations especially seem to like this collegial environment and the group energy that comes with working surrounded by others. They can choose to either put on earphones and not be interrupted or communicate easily with their peers and bosses when they need to. Companies are finding that this new configuration promotes the collaboration that is so important to modern work styles.

## COLLABORATIVE ENVIRONMENTS

The term for this sort of workspace is "hybrid environment." In addition to open space where employees' desks are located, some offices now have shared areas to accommodate virtual and temporary project-based workers, as well as spaces that appeal to more casual working styles. Forward-thinking companies integrate meeting space with advanced technology so teams can meet electronically — "touchdown" spaces where temporary or visiting workers can plug in, and more relaxed settings such as lounges.

Organizations are moving to this more informal workspace structure because they see the advantages that group collaboration brings to their bottom lines. According to a 2007 Gartner research study, employees now spend 70 percent of their time working in groups — up 10 percent than they did 10 years earlier. And with research showing that collective intelligence outperforms individual reasoning, this trend is expected to continue.

## Virtual Meeting Rooms

Videoconferencing rooms are an important part of collaborative trends, and they're changing pretty dramatically to comfortably accommodate global work teams. Instead of videoconferencing's being a very stiff situation in which you sit in front of a screen, looking straight ahead, new virtual meeting rooms are being built as immersive environments with multiangle HD cameras, large media screens, interactive white boards, and plug-ins at each station so participants can share information from their laptops. People can stand or sit, even walk around the room, and they're always visible to the group onscreen, at life size. Some of the systems even make it look like all the participants are sitting around a large round table together.

In some ways, these virtual spaces can be more engaging than an in-person meeting. Having that video camera on and knowing someone is watching changes one's performance. It's also a lot more comfortable and productive to meet this way than it would be via audioconference or traditional videoconferencing—especially for a long meeting. With facetime and skype now available on pda's, workers in the field, on a train, or on a site inspection can now be visually connected to those sitting at HQ.

## OTHER ELECTRONIC TOOLS

Introduction of any new technology needs to involve research, training, and a capital expenditure. For those who don't have the capital to invest in virtual meeting rooms — and in an IBM study, only 21 percent of the human resource professionals interviewed said their company had invested in collaborative or networking tools recently — the use of other, less-expensive electronic tools is sure to grow.

Community forums for information are increasingly entering the scene — websites where people can interact with one another or with a knowledge base that indexes what questions are most often asked and responds with up-to-the-moment information; wikis where people can post, edit, and add to information that will be shared with either internal or external audiences; and social networking sites where companies can interact with customers, potential employees, and work teams. Though in the past businesses have been leery of these communication options, thinking they offer poor information, waste time, or are a confidentiality minefield, this seems to be changing. Whether or not wikis and social networking will replace intranets is up for debate, but as people get more comfortable with these tools, they're likely to become more common.

Still, regardless of what forms of electronic interaction companies are using, they'll never completely replace face-to-face communication. A mix of in-person interaction and technological, with different tools used for different needs, will continue to be the norm. The most successful and thorough communication is still achieved in person with coworkers and clients.

## TEMPORARY WORKERS

Large corporations have been trending toward using temporary workers — contract workers, short-term workers, and project-based workers — for quite a while. A report by the labor law firm Littler Mendelson predicts that contingent workers could soon make up 30 percent to 50 percent of the entire U.S. workforce. Human resource professionals are building staffing plans that integrate temporary workers as a consistent part of teams, according to IBM's report "Working Beyond Borders." Some of these freelancers are working virtually, others have a desk at the employer's office, but regardless, this new model is presenting challenges.

The ramp-up time required for temporary workers to learn the ropes at a new company is a big hurdle. So are the lag time and hurdles experienced by workers in identifying with the corporate culture, feeling part of a team, and understanding how to access company resources. Hiring temporary workers is also causing more work for managers, who must help freelancers acclimate. So where do I see this headed? I think we'll see more niche agencies designed to place freelancers based on industry skill set and knowledge rather than the more generalized temp agencies we've been used to; I'm already seeing this happen in industries such as online advertising, programming, software development, and other digital-oriented companies.

We can also count on there being additional learning resources to get temporary workers up to speed. New technologies will definitely be a part of this, according to IBM's report: social media so workers can share insights and resources, and even the use of virtual learning environments where they can immerse themselves in the culture and shorten that learning curve.

## TABLETS

So far, I've talked mainly about channels of communication — videoconferencing, social networking, wikis — but what about the hardware people use to connect? That, too, may be changing in the next few years.

Forrester Research estimates that fifty-nine million tablets, such as iPad and Kindle will have been purchased by the end of 2015. And we are already seeing signs that many of them will not be strictly for personal use, but will be showing up in a workplace near you.

In certain industries, especially those that require information to be portable, tablets are starting to replace laptops and paper documents. This has been especially true in the health care field, for people who travel to their customers or clients rather than the other way around, and for those in transportation such as pilots. Numerous hospitals, financial and insurance companies such as Lloyd's of London and even U.S. federal agencies are testing tablets for possible use. But there are two big issues at hand when it comes to tablets: security and compatibility. When a tablet contains information as sensitive as medical records, financial accounts, and flight plans, you don't want to lose it or have it stolen without knowing the information on it is secure. Because different tablets use different operating systems, compatibility is also an issue companies are looking into to see how they can integrate these new handheld devices into their larger IT program.

## SECURITY AND PRIVACY

What I predict will be the biggest continuing trend of all in the future is our concern about security and privacy. Everything I've discussed in this chapter circles back to that issue: virtual meetings going out over the network, increased use of public social forums, expanded integration of temporary workers and more portable devices that can be stolen or left on the bus. As companies move from private servers and off-the-shelf software to cloud computing, the security and privacy risk increases more and more. I see this as the biggest communication issue of the next five years.

There are also privacy issues because of the new way people work—in other words, beyond the hours of nine to five. A Wordpress article speaks to this directly: "While most employers maintain that you leave your privacy rights at the door or the workplace, particularly when the use of company communications equipment is involved, employees counter that portable technology has increasingly blurred the line between our work and personal lives, and that it is unreasonable to expect workers to monitor and censor their communication at all times."

Privacy touches all levels of corporate communication, from the individual employee to the organization as a whole. How this will play itself out, only time will tell. What we do know is that information, senders, and receivers must be protected, no matter what the communication channel.

\* \* \*

Which brings us back to where we started, to that simple equation: communication involves a sender, receiver, message, and channel. Though there are many complications surrounding each component, one of the best tips I can offer is to keep the sender, receiver, message, and channel in mind each time you communicate and don't forget to **confirm** with the receiver that each message has been communicated the way you intended.

The modern day workplace poses a number of new considerations regarding communication. Success will involve planning, organization, and a willingness to adjust and embrace the changes as they happen.

## ONE FINAL THOUGHT

As George Bernard Shaw suggested more than fifty years ago,

"The problem with communication..is the illusion that is has been successfully accomplished."

By not only sending and receiving information, but by confirming the accuracy of the transmission, communication in the modern workplace will be optimized and productivity increased.

# REFERENCES

## Chapter 1: Helping You Find Your Way

Blalock, Marty. "Listen Up: Why Good Communication Is Good Business." *Wisconsin Business Alumni Update.* Winter 2005.

Braedyn Svecz, Amanda-Makenzie. "Basic Elements and Tips to Build Effective Workplace Communication." September 26, 2010. http://www.suite101.com/content/basic-elements–tips-to-build-effective-workplace-communication-a290104.

"Business Communication and Its Types." July 21, 2010. http://lawyercommunication.blogspot.com.

## Chapter 2: Information Overload

Amble, Brian. "Information Overload Suffocating Managers." *Management Issues.* January 5, 2007.

Fried, Ina. "Driven to Distraction by Technology." *CNET News.* July 21, 2005. http://news.cnet.com/Driven-to-distraction-by-technology/2100-1022_3-5797028.html.

"How Cell-Phone Radiation Works." (n.d.) http://electronics.howstuffworks.com/cell-phone-radiation2.htm.

Lickerman, Alex. "The Effect of Technology on Relationships." *Psychology Today*, June 2010.

Mann, Martin. "Inbox Zero: Articles of Faith." March 13, 2006. http://www.43folders.com/2006/03/13/philosophy.

Rock, David. *Your Brain at Work*. New York: Harper Business, 2009.

"Ten Tips to Avoid Information Overload at Work." September 9, 2008. http://bytes.com/topic/management/insights/836461-10-tips-avoid-information-overload-work#post3344623.

Thompson, Clive. "Meet the Life Hackers." *New York Times*. October 16, 2005.

Van Winkle, William. "Information Overload." (n.d.) http://www.gdrc.org/icts/i-overload/infoload.html.

Young, Richard. "Five Tips for Surviving Information Overload." August 17, 2010. http://www.techrepublic.com/blog/five-tips/five-tips-for-surviving-information-overload/247.

Zeldes, Nathan. "Infoglut." *IEEE Spectrum* 46 (10) October 2009.

## Chapter 3: E-Mail: The Most Used and Abused Form of Communication

Bernstein, Elizabeth. "Reply All: The Button Everyone Loves to Hate." *Wall Street Journal*. March 8, 2011.

Brenner, Leslie. "In(sane)-Box." *Los Angeles Times*. July 31, 2008.

Brogan, Chris. "Writing More Effective E-mail." February 19, 2008. http://www.chrisbrogan. com/writing-more-effective-email/.

Carr, Austin. "Open Thread: The End of Email?" *Fast Company.* June 17, 2010.

The Creative Group. "Marketing Execs' Most Embarrassing Email Mistakes." July 10, 2009. http://www.marketingcharts.com/interactive/ marketing-execs-most-embarrassing-e-mail- mistakes-9742/.

Fallows, Deborah. "E-mail at Work." December 8, 2010. http://www.pewinternet.org/Reports/ 2002/E-mail-at-work.aspx.

Jertz, Dennis B., and Jessica Bauer. "Writing Effective E-mail: Top Ten Tips." March 8, 2011. http:// jerz.setonhill.edu/writing/e-text/e-mail/.

Jones, Del. "When You've Got Too Much E-mail." *USA Today.* January 4, 2002Lohrmann, Dan. "Too Much E-mail? Survey Results Say Yes." July 19, 2010. http://www.govtechblogs.com/ lohrmann_on_infrastructure/2010/07/too- much-e-mail-new-survey-resu.php.

Luhn, Robert. "D'oh! The Most Disastrous E-mail Mistakes." *PC World.* April 29, 2002.

Mayfield, Ross. "E-mail Hell." October 16, 2008. http://ross.typepad.com/blog/2008/10/ e-mail-hell.html.

Noguchi, Yuki. "Make It Stop! Crushed by Too Many E-Mails." NPR. June 16, 2008. http://www.npr.org/templates/story/story. php?storyId=91366853.

Su, Tina. "15 Tips for Writing Effective E-mails." November 2008. http://thinksimplenow.com/ productivity/15-tips-for-writing-effective-e-mail/.

Tschabitscher, Heinz. "How Many E-mails Are Sent Every Day?" http://e-mail.about.com/od/e-mailtrivia/f/e-mails_per_day.htm.

## Chapter 4: Communicating Across Generations

AARP. "Leading a Multigenerational Workforce." 2007.

Fertik, Michael. "Managing Employees in Their Twenties." *Harvard Business Review*. January 21, 2011.

Hammill, Greg. "Mixing and Managing Four Generations of Employees." *FDU Magazine Online*. Winter/Spring 2009. http://www.fdu.edu/newspubs/magazine/05ws/generations.htm.

Kersten, Denise. "Today's Generations Face New Communications Gaps." *USA Today*. November 15, 2002.

"Survey Finds Workplace Technology Etiquette Blurred Between Generations." (n.d.) http://itmanagersinbox.com/1265/survey-finds-workplace-technology-etiquette-blurred-between-generations/.

Tolbize, Anick. "Generational Differences in the Workplace." University of Minnesota Research and Training Center on Community Living. August 16, 2008.

## Chapter 5: The Virtual Worker Challenge

Broda, Karen, and Rebecca Hinkle. "Five Tips for Better Virtual Meetings." *Harvard Management Update* 13 (3).

Citrix Online. "When You Can't Meet Face to Face: Connecting Today's Global Businesses. (Webcast).

Citrix Online. "Cut Costs and Drive Efficiency of Virtual Teams." January 6, 2009. http://www.computerworld.com/pdfs/Citrix_Cut_Costs.pdf.

Exforsys. "Virtual Team Communication," April 30, 2009. http://www.exforsys.com/career-center/virtual-team/virtual-team-communication.html.

Manpower. "The World of Virtual Work: Facts and Statistics." (n.d.) http://files.shareholder.com/downloads/MAN/164668571x0x117500/bcbbb96d-64a8-4a24-a3ab-1a41ecffb7db/MP_World%20of%20Virtual%20Work%20Facts_Stats_FINAL.pdf.

Pisani, Joseph. "Workplace BlackBerry Use May Spur Lawsuits." July 9, 2008. http://www.cnbc.com/id/25586129/Workplace_BlackBerry_Use_May_Spur_Lawsuits.

"Telework Trendlines 2009: A Survey Brief by WorldatWork." February 2009. http://www.workingfromanywhere.org/news/Trendlines_2009.pdf.

Thompson, Margot. "7 Steps to Exceptional Virtual Team Communication." February 3, 2010. http://www.ceoconsultant.com/business/7-steps-exceptional-virtual-team-communication/

**Chapter 6: Globalization**

Blalock, Marty. "Listen Up: Why Good Communication Is Good Business." *Wisconsin Business Alumni Update*. Winter 2005.

Kwintessential.co.uk. "The Tips for Cross Cultural Communication." http://www.kwintessential.co.uk/cultural-services/articles/ten-tips-cross-cultural-communication.html.

The Levin Institute (State University of New York). *Globalization 101: A Student's Guide to Globalizationi*. http://www.globalization101.org.

Sewell, John. "Challenges of Globalization." *Human Rights Dialogue* 1, no. 11, Summer 1998.

Mielke, David. "Effective Global Communication Requires Cross-Cultural Sensitivity." September 20, 2009. http://www.annarbor.com/business-review/effective-global-communication-requires-cross-cultural-sensitivity/

Reynolds, Sana, and Deborah Valentine, *Guide to Cross-Cultural Communication*, 2nd Ed. (Upper Saddle River, NJ: Prentice Hall, 2010).

RW3. The Culture Wizard. http://rw-3.com.

Walker, Robyn. *Strategic Business Communication: An Integrated, Ethical Approach*, 1st Ed. (Los Angeles: University of Southern California Press, 2006).

## Chapter 7: The Future of Communication

Steelcase. "Distributed Collaboration: Work's Future in View." *360°* 61.

Challenger, Gray & Christmas. "New Report Predicts Rise of Contingent Workforce." *HR Issues*. April 20, 2010.

"Workplace Privacy Rights on the Docket." *HR Issues*. April 20, 2010.

Claburn, Thomas. "iPad Leads Tablets into Workplace." *InformationWeek*. October 27, 2010.

Diana, Alison. "Executives Demand Communications Arsenal." *InformationWeek*. September 30, 2010.

IBM. "Working Beyond Borders: Insights from the Global Chief Human Resource Study." 2010.

Laing, Andrew. "What Will the Future Workplace Look Like?" *CNN Money*. January 19, 2011.

Lipowicz, Alice. "Federal Workplace to Rely More on Mobile, Panelists Say." *Federal Computer Week*. June 24, 2011.

Porter, Alan. "Wikis in the Workplace: A Practical Introduction." *ARSTechnica*. November 16, 2009.

Shewchuk, Ron. "Social Media Have a Role to Play in the Workplace." *The Vancouver Sun*. March 18, 2010.

Violino, Bob. "Invited or Not, Tablets Are Coming to Your Workplace." *Government Health IT*. August 18, 2011.

11474265R00074

Made in the USA
Charleston, SC
27 February 2012